52 WAYS TO IGNITE
YOUR CONGREGATION . . .

YOUTH MINISTRY

**52**

# WAYS TO IGNITE
# YOUR CONGREGATION . . .
## YOUTH MINISTRY

STEVEN CASE

THE
PILGRIM
PRESS
Cleveland

The Pilgrim Press
700 Prospect Avenue
Cleveland, Ohio 44115
thepilgrimpress.com

© 2012 by The Pilgrim Press

Library of Congress Cataloging-in-Publication Data

Case, Steve L., 1964–
    Youth ministry / Steven Case.
        p.    cm – (52 ways to ignite your congregation)
    ISBN 978-0-8298-1884-0 (alk. paper)
    1. Church group work with youth.   I. Title.
  BV4447.C3794 2012
  259'.23 – dc23

                                    2012005105

# Contents

# ❶

# Youth Ministry Is a Calling

I have been in youth ministry for twenty-two years. That's *twenty-two years* of youth ministry. The last ten have been as a commissioned minister and licensed minister with the United Church of Christ. I have baptized youth. I have given them communion. I have buried them. I have held their hands at funerals. I have had late night online chats with youth as their parents scream hateful words at each other in the next room. I have lost (and won) many belching contests, have driven through hundreds of drive-throughs, eaten hundreds of pizzas, lost my temper, been pelted with snowballs, and held a weeping student in my arms and lied that it would be all better soon.

And still I have people come up to me and say, "So, when are you going to be a real minister?"

Youth ministers *are* real ministers.

Youth ministry is a calling.

In my opinion, it is the highest of callings.

Years ago, just a few years after I started this line of work, I attended one of those national youth worker conferences. We're talking about three to five thousand youth ministers all in one place and all simultaneously coming unglued.

The creators of the conference played a game. They made everyone in the room stand on their chairs. The host began to count, 1 . . . 2 . . . 3 . . . 4 . . . when he reached the number of years that each of us had been in youth ministry, we were to sit down. By the time he reached ten most of the room was seated. 11 . . . 12 . . . 13 . . . he kept counting. When he reached forty, there were two people still standing. At forty-one, one of those two sat down and then, as one body, the rest of the room rose up and gave the last person a standing ovation. She had been in youth ministry for forty-seven years—*as a volunteer!*

This is a calling.

You must understand that or the rest of this book isn't going to make much of a difference.

**TIP #1: Youth ministry is real ministry.**

## 2

# Celebrate the Youth You Have

So you're standing in the vestibule of the church, worship is over, and everyone is sipping coffee out of paper cups. Perfectly well meaning people will come up to you and say the one phrase youth ministers can't stand: "So how many kids are showing up on a Sunday night?"

No, these people are not being judgmental; they are just making conversation. But for too many churches the only method of judging a program's success is by the number of butts in the chairs on Sunday night.

Have you ever noticed that when people look back fondly on the good old days, the number of youth who used to be in the church tends to grow. If you have twenty students people will look thoughtful for a moment, turn to a friend, and say, "Do you remember back when we had seventy or eighty kids here on a Sunday night." (If you said you had fifty they would remember back when there were more than a hundred. Don't let it get to you.)

**TIP #2: The Kingdom of God is your canvas; teenagers are your paint. See the colors God gave you to work with.**

# 3

# Youth Ministry Occurs
# in Groups of One

Youth ministry is not about having fifty students playing Shuffle Your Buns in the church on a Sunday night. Youth ministry occurs in the *one.*

Imagine it's a Thursday night, and the youth minister is sitting on a hard plastic chair in a high school auditorium watching the worst production of *A Music Man* in the history of American educational theater. Harold Hill is fourteen, and his voice has not changed. He hasn't hit the right note yet. The set has fallen over twice, and the piano teacher can't play. The youth minister sits through this because *one* of his students said, "I have a solo this year. Would you come?"

The youth minister knows that dad is in and out of the student's life. Mom is working two jobs to make ends meet, and it is very likely that neither will be able to make any of the three performances.

The young lady sings her solo (which turns out to be two lines during the Wells Fargo number), and then she's back in the chorus. The youth minister sits through both acts because she knows that when the curtain call happens, the brave student is going to be looking to see if her youth minister is there. That is youth ministry.

Youth ministry occurs late at night on the winter retreat when the lessons have been taught, the smores have been eaten, and the shoes and socks are drying by the fire. *One* student will come up and say, "Could I talk to you about something?" That is youth ministry.

Youth ministry occurs when that *one* student gets a text message that simply says, "You go girl" minutes before she walks into the midterm that she was studying for instead of going to church on Sunday night. That is youth ministry.

The games, the lessons, the events, the retreats, the lock-ins—all of that is the candy that surrounds the Tootsie Roll center of the Tootsie Pop. The connection between the students and their creator, more often than not, is going to occur *one* on *one*.

More and Bigger are not listed among the fruits of the spirit. Patience, Kindness, Compassion, and Love are.

**TIP #3: Youth ministry usually occurs when there aren't many people around.**

**4**

# The 10 Percent Solution

There are numbers people in this world. Some people must have a chart and a spreadsheet to make an accurate assessment of a program's success in order to have something on the agenda for their job review. For those people, a late night conversation driving home from the amusement park isn't going to count when deciding whether to increase the youth budget.

Short and sweet, if your church has a hundred people sitting in the congregation on Sunday morning, a youth program of ten students is perfectly acceptable. If you are going to count the number of people in the church membership directory, then you must also count the number of students the youth minister has as friends on Facebook, the number of students she has in her cell phone, and the number of Tweets she is following. By the way, if you're not sure what Facebook or Tweets are, well, we'll talk about those later.

The 10 Percent Rule is a valid measuring stick. If you have a hundred people show up on Sunday for church and your youth group hovers around twenty, good for you! If your youth group hovers around five, then you might want to look into marketing it a little better.

**TIP #4: Sunday night attendance should be about 10 percent or more of the congregation.**

**5**

# Go Where the Youth Are

Wherever two or three youths are gathered, that is your office. Here's a conversation played out in churches across the country (regardless of religion or denomination).

CHURCH ELDER TYPE: Why are you never in your office?

YOUTH MINISTER: There are no youth in my office.

CHURCH ELDER TYPE: Yes, but if you spent more time in your office the teenagers would know where to find you.

YOUTH MINISTER: It's easier for me to go find them. I can meet them at Starbucks or someplace.

CHURCH ELDER TYPE: But if they came to you, you wouldn't have to leave the building.

YOUTH MINISTER: Why would they come to me? I'm never in my office.

CHURCH ELDER TYPE: (*sighs heavily and pinches the bridge of her nose*).

A youth minister's office is Starbucks or Caribou or whatever coffee shop is nearby. The office is the skate park. Often the office is sitting in front of the computer commenting on every student's Facebook post. (There's that word again.) Yes there's a computer in the youth minister's office, but most likely the one she has at home is better. Heck, most likely the one she has in her pocket is better than the one in her office. (*Note to the memorial committee*: A plaque on the wall or a plant in the garden won't win nearly as many hearts to Jesus as a laptop for the youth leader.)

Keeping youth ministers in their office is like grounding teen-agers to their room. It's punishment.

You'll see much better results in the program if you don't see the youth ministers stuck behind their desks.

**TIP #5: Wherever two or three (youth) are gathered, there is the youth minister.**

## 6

# Youth Ministry Is Loud

Here are two words that mean "become silent." They are Greek words found in the scriptures: *sige* (see-gay) and *sigao* (see-gah-oh)

*Sige is* the word Jesus said to the storm and to the crazy naked guy who ran around around the tombs yelling at graves. It means "shhhhh" or "hush." It is said in the way you would speak to a small child crying in the night during a thunderstorm. The other word, *sigao,* is much angrier.

I became fascinated by the way that the words translated into Greek could change the meaning of the situation.

If we take the phrase "youth ministry," not the individual words "youth" and "ministry," but the term "youth ministry" and translate that backward, in the same way we learn that the term in the ancient Greek language means "messy noise." (Okay, that's not true. I made that up completely, but it's one of those things that *should* be true.)

Youth ministry is often loud, ordinarily annoying, as a rule messy, universally unglamorous, customarily disgusting, repeatedly boisterous, routinely disorderly, often smelly, frequently vulgar, seldom peaceful, and more often than not dangerous.

Why do so many churches treat youth ministry as if it's just another part of Sunday school? Churches and church leaders must recognize that it takes a special kind of leader and a special kind of church to make a youth program work.

Here's a question: *When Jesus broke wind did it smell like strawberries?*

If your committee can't get beyond the idea that the son of God may have actually broken wind on occasion, then you're going to have a hard time supporting a youth ministry program.

Trust the youth leaders. They are following a very special kind of calling. Youth ministry will never fit into the box that most churches want to fit it into (not without it leaking something gross on the carpet). Allow youth ministry to be loud and messy. Welcome it. You will be amazed how a program can grow when youth are given permission to be who they are and are not asked to fit into the preconceived ideas of a committee.

**TIP #6: Youth ministry is a lot like kindergarten.**

**7**

# God Calls All Types to Ministry

WANTED: YOUTH MINISTER: Must be white, male, play guitar, have a goatee, wear a Hawaiian shirt, and know all the words to *Monty Python and the Holy Grail.*

Once upon a time there was this mean old bastard named Saul. God called him and used him to share the message. After God changed his name, he wrote the majority of the New Testament.

Once upon a time there was a giant killer, shepherd, street musician, dancer, and voyeur named David. God called him and used him to build his church.

Once upon a time there was a crazy older lady name Sally, who at age sixty-eight went to the youth director and said, "I'd like to help chaperone the mission trip."

Churches tend to think they need to connect with teens by bringing in the cool guy with the shaved head who can sing and play every song U2 ever wrote.

More than anything else teenagers need to have a leader who is *authentic.* Teenagers can spot a fake from a mile away. If your leader is trying to show the youth how cool he or she is, the youth will eat him or her alive.

Youth need to be shown realness in their leaders. People who are flawed and uncool. People who know who they are and accept themselves and love themselves. Youth respond to the authentic better than they respond to the cool.

Don't worry that your students never listen to you; worry that they are always watching you.

**TIP #7: God calls whomever God wants to call.**

# 8

## Mountain Dew Is a Youth Ministry Tool

What do all these things have in common: finger paint, Oreos, duct tape, artificial snow, Mountain Dew, sidewalk chalk, peanut butter, one gross of rubber bouncy balls, M&M's, and a website with a collection of proverbs from fortune cookies? Give up? These are all items from a youth minister's monthly shopping list.

Youth ministry is about going to creative, if not outright extreme, means to meet Jesus.

Youth ministers do not think like normal people. You may pick up a box of Frosted Cheerios in the store and think breakfast. A youth worker will think, "If we put a Cheerio up somebody's nose and then had them blow it out on a table that I set up to look like a football field, we have a game to play this Sunday."

One of the best gifts I received recently was the discovery of eight twelve-packs of soda pop; each pack was almost two years past the expiration date. They could not have been consumed without teens getting sick. But you can't throw away eight twelve-packs. I gave each student a can of soda, and we went out into the parking lot. The students each had to talk about a time in the last week when they were so stressed or angry or excited they thought they might burst. Then they were to shake the can and throw it as high as they could.

Youth ministry will never be like Sunday school. It requires a completely different way of thinking as well as a completely different shopping list.

**TIP #8: Whatever you can use to get teens closer to God is a legitimate tool for ministry.**

# 9

## Change Is a Good Thing

One of the greatest games ever invented in youth ministry is called Sardines. It's something like Hide & Seek, but it uses the whole church building. One person goes out to hide, and everyone else must seek the hiding person. Here's the catch: when you find the hiding person you hide with that person; hence the name Sardines. (How many teenagers can you fit into the janitor's mop closet?)

It's a great game. I have played it for years, teaching it to groups of various denominations across the country. In my program it has morphed into something new. Now when the students go to hide, they must hide and then text someone back in the youth room (home base). The hiding person must continue to text the rest of the group until they are found.

Youth ministry is about change. Everything changes. Nothing, and I mean this from the bottom of my schoolboy's heart, *nothing* can kill a program quicker than "We've never done it that way before."

Change is good. Sometimes change must happen for the sake of change. You don't have a Christmas wreath sale because you *always* have a Christmas wreath sale. The way we've always done it destroys the opportunity for new people to come in and feel welcome. The way we've always done it creates cliques, causes boredom, and disallows creativity.

Allowing for change, encouraging change, teaches teens adaptability, opens them to new ideas, keeps them on their toes, and puts a stop to complacency.

Would you attend a program on a regular basis if you knew exactly what was going to happen when you got there? What if every time you went something different happened? What if every mission trip was to someplace new instead of the same place you went last year?

**TIP #9: Keep your youth guessing, and you will keep them coming back.**

**10**

# Ignite Your Youth Ministry Program by Igniting Your Youth Minister

One of the greatest compliments I ever received as a youth minister came fairly on in my career. The mother of one of my students gave my baby daughter a cabbage patch doll as a Christmas gift. (This is back at a time when people were beating each other up for cabbage patch dolls.) I was completely taken aback. I asked, "Why did you do this?"

She said, "I have a fifteen-year-old daughter, and last week she fought me because she *wanted* to go to church, and I was too tired to take her. I figure," she said, "that I owe you at least this much."

I once got a Certificate of Appreciation from a church where I was working. It was printed out by the secretary, someone put a gold sticker on it, and it was signed by the head of the administrative board. Everyone on the staff got one.

Yippee! Nothing says we appreciate you like a dollar store frame.

If you are going to appreciate your youth ministers, then *appreciate* them. Give them a gift card to Starbucks or their favorite coffee shop. Give them a restaurant certificate so they can have dinner with a spouse someplace other than where they must order their food out of a clown's mouth. Do you have more than a hundred people in your church? Could you go to them and say, "Would you be willing to buy the youth minister a cup of coffee?"(Hopefully most of them would say yes.) Collect that money, and buy your youth leaders a gift card so that every Sunday they begin their workday feeling appreciated.

Say thank you once in awhile. Acknowledge what they go through, what they sacrifice, what they accomplish. Youth ministry is a game of seed planting. Youth ministers seldom see the fruits of their labor.

Find a collection of thirty people who will make a commitment to simply pray for the youth minister every day. Not necessarily for the youth program but for the youth *leader*.

Support your youth ministers with a budget. Give them the money they need to do their job. How many other programs in the church have to raise their own funds? Do you see the Ladies Quilting Circle having a car wash? Does the choir need to have a yard work weekend to buy music?

I bet if you asked, you would find that your church's youth leaders spend a considerable amount of money out of their own pockets every year because one or seven of the youth forgot her money on movie day. Seek out individual members of the congregation, and ask them to purchase movie gift cards and McDonalds gift certificates and other such gift cards from local youth hang outs. The next time someone says, "I forgot my money. Will you buy me a hamburger?" not only will the minister be able to do so but will feel supported at the same time.

Perhaps the key to supporting your youth ministers is to do so *continuously*. Not just once a year on Staff Appreciation Day, but all the time. Make a point to pat them on the back. Send goofy emails of babies laughing. Send a joke. Put a happy meal toy in their mailbox. Xerox your face, and put the copy on their office door.

Set a goal as a church, as a family of God, that Staff Appreciation Day is unnecessary because the staff already knows they are appreciated.

**TIP #10: Love your youth minister as much as God does.**

# Welcome Youth

It may seem obvious, but it's amazing how many times churches will say they want to welcome teenagers when what they really want is to have lots of teens—*over there.*

Teenagers are the end result of childhood. Sunday school too often happens far away from the sanctuary in another hall or sometimes another building. Many churches have fought the battle of children's church and whether children should be in the sanctuary.

Once children reach the age of twelve, the congregation suddenly expects them to magically be interested in coming to worship services and other church activities. Why? Up until now they have been placed with the youngest members of the church.

If we want to *ignite* a youth program, then we must *invite* youth. Ask specific members of your congregation to invite teens to sit with them. Invite youth to your church's version of a Ladies Quilting Circle or Men's Garden Club. If the men's group in your church has an annual pancake breakfast, invite some of the guys from the youth Sunday school—not to do the dishes but to be a part of the event.

If we want teens to be an active part of the life of the church, then the life of the church must invite them.

**TIP #11: Teenagers must feel welome if they are to come back.**

# ⑫

# Mission Trips Are About Sending, Not Going

I remember being a kid in church. Every now and then there would be an All Church Chili Lunch or Pancake Supper or some other congregational event. One of the many missionaries sponsored by the denomination would come in with a slide projector and show us all pictures of villages in far-off places that we could not pronounce. We would look at sweating mission workers digging a well, building a school, or giving an immunization injection to a kid who was crying as a mission worker comforted him. Our church would then pass the plate, and we would send the missionary on his way to the next church well funded to continue his life-saving work. I remember when the youth group of this same church wanted to send a team to a rural area of our own country to help insulate people's homes, put on a new roof, or dig a well, and the congregation asked, "When are you going to have the car wash and bake sale to pay for this?

We need to rethink how we as the church pay for mission trips. This is mission. This is a group of young people who want to answer the call of God and be the hands, feet, eyes, ears, and heart of Jesus Christ. The natural assumption is not, "How are you going to pay for it?" It should be, "How much do you need?"

**TIP #12: The youth group should not be thinking, "How do we raise the money so we can go?" The congregation should be thinking, "How do we raise the money so we can send?"**

# ⓭

# Mission Trips
# Should Not Be Local

There is something about being away from home that changes your perspective on the world. All of us have driven home and passed the man on the street with the cardboard sign that says, "Hungry." It's different when you are sitting next to him in a shelter. It's different when you think about how exactly he is going to keep warm tonight when it gets cold. These thoughts don't make as much of an impact when you can go home every night if the mom-and-dad safety net is there to catch you, to say it's going to be okay. Then we aren't really experiencing the mission *trip*.

If you undertake a local mission trip, there will always be someone who comes late or has to take off during the day for a dentist appointment or a well-meaning mother who wants to come along to make sure nothing is too upsetting. Take your students away on a mission trip, and they have no choice but to deal with what they see. They must struggle with weariness. They have no choice but to put their heart and soul into the work. Of course there are always charities and organizations in our own communities that need help and volunteers. Mission work can be local. Anytime during the year students can help out and give their time, but a mission *trip* must involve travel. Moreover, those who go on a mission trip are much more likely to volunteer their time when they return.

**TIP #13: Mission trips should require a suitcase.**

# 14

## Mission Trips Are
## About Making Disciples

Jesus took a group of rag-tag followers and turned them into extensions of him. He sent them into the world with the instructions to do as he did. When we take teenagers on mission trips, we come home with pictures or videos and stories about what they did and who the met. The pictures are evidence that work was done, but they don't show how lives where changed. Sure, you can see the smiling person with a group of sweaty teens in front of her house with the new roof. You can say, "See? Her life was changed. She has a new roof on her house. We made a difference." But you can't always see the work and the change that was done in the teenager's soul. Mission trips are about becoming the hands of Christ. Mission trips are only partially about the work that gets done. Mission trips create disciples. We must teach our students that Jesus Christ is alive and well and fully present in this place because *they* are. They are Christ's hands. they are Christ's eyes, feet, ears, heart, and voice.

I took a group of teens to a poverty-stricken area of the country where they spent a week insulating a man's home for the upcoming harsh winter. The entire week the man sat on his front porch and sipped his beer. Many of my students began to grow resentful. Why are we helping him if he isn't even going to help himself? The minister on the trip took the time that evening and told my students about *agape*. Loving the way Jesus loved. The Bible does not say "Love each other as long as... It says, Love each other. Love without any expectation of getting anything in return. Just love." Hard to do. Harder to understand? Of course. Did it challenge the youth of that trip? Absolutely. Did they learn something about Jesus without ever cracking open the Bible? Sure. Did they learn what it means to give of themselves? Yes. Were they changed? Permanently. There was a mission trip T-shirt I saw that said, Rebuilding homes. Rebuilding lives. A beautiful mission statement if ever there was one. But let us remember that the lives being rebuilt are also the ones wearing the shirts.

**TIP #14: Mission trips change everyone's life: the receivers and the givers.**

# 15

# Mission Trips
# Are Not Vacation

I took a group of teens on a GREEN-Mission trip. Our original goal was to see if we could help clean up the gulf oil spill in 2010. There is a great deal of training involved and age restrictions so we could not work there, but my group wanted to do something go green for our summer mission project. We found an organization that was rebuilding an oyster reef. In the next hundred years or so the artificial reef would connect with the natural existing reef and provide habitat for various forms of wildlife while also preserving the eco-system and protecting the area from coastal erosion. We were on an island, sleeping on the floor of a local church. We were working in a bog, often up to our waists in mud and muck. Rebuilding a reef involves hauling thirty-five pound biodegradable bags of shells that cut and scratch. By the end of the day the smell of sweat and bug spray and muck is overpowering. The first Sunday after we got home one of our church members asked me, "So how was your week at the beach?"

Teenagers are willing to give up a week of their summer vacation, often a week of earning money, so they can go and be a servant of God. A funny thing happens when you say, "Here I am God, send me" (the way Isaiah did). God may send you to some pretty scary places. Any youth willing to participate get the praise and respect of the congregation.

TIP #15: Vacations are a get-away. Mission trips are more of a "Get-to."

**16**

# To Hear God's Voice We Must Be Willing to Shut Up and Listen

Silence is a great way to connect with something bigger than yourself.

Whether you work with teenagers or are a teenager, yourself, there is great power in silence. Have you ever asked a group of teens a question during discussion time and get back nothing but silence? What happens when you let that silence hang? It gets so thick it's almost tangible. What if you could make that silence work for you? What if you could create a place where students could do nothing but listen for the whisper of God?

You can plan great retreats or camping weekends, but the moments that truly make a difference on these outings is the time around the campfire. There is a power in those final moments before bed when you read a story by flashlight.

There is a time and place for cell phones and iPods. There is also a time and place for silence and listening. Plan a lock-in or retreat where the students do not get to take along their phones and other electronic equipment. You'll hear loud protests because for most of them it's like putting duct tape over their mouths (or in some cases their fingers.) Ask them in the beginning what they listen for? Have they ever listened so hard that you could almost hear them listen?

When you are left with only your own company it's amazing how much you find out about yourself. Convince your students to try a cell-quiet weekend just once. It will be maddening for some and liberating for others, but the lesson of solitude will not go unlearned.

Do you have a closet in the youth room? Perhaps a small storage space where you put all the equipment for games? There is a reason Jesus suggested going into your prayer closet. There is a time for corporate (group) prayer, a time when the simple act of praying connects us with others. There is also a time to shut out the world and just be with God. Clutter cuts us off. Silence can open us up to the movement of the Holy Spirit.

**TIP #16: Sometimes God whispers; learn to listen closely.**

# Simplify Simplify Simplify
### —Henry David Thoreau

A few years back I was trying to find a curriculum that would last several weeks. I found a video series I thought would work. Good music. Cool graphics. Built-in discussion guide. I played it for my youth, and they rebelled on the first night. Apparently, it was the same sort of lesson videos the school was using to teach. They didn't want to show up on Sundays and get another school lesson.

Students are bombarded with technology during the week. Most of them live plugged in. Let the youth room be a technology free zone. Take cell phones as they come through the door. (Give them back, of course.) No TV, no boom box, no laptop visuals just talk. Read from an actual Bible. Create games out of the flotsam and jetsam that you find in the supply closet. Create a sanctuary away from the bombarding messages of the outside world. Some of the best meetings I've had in twenty-two years of youth ministry have been when the props, gadgets, players, or equipment has blown, broken, or busted, and we are left with nothing but an opportunity to sit on the floor and talk about life.

This generation accepts texting as conversation. But a strange thing happens when you take away the impersonal-ness of conversation. You start to appreciate a face-to-face conversation. Seeing a person's face and watching a person's reaction is a requirement for real communication. A hand on your shoulder, a comforting tone in your voice, a sympathetic look, and the ability to simply look at someone and know you are being heard —not read but actually heard—opens doors into students' lives that spend way too much time closed.

I once had my students leading worship on Good Friday. We read Psalm 23 aloud, but I had the students surround the congregation. Each student started the reading one verse behind the next creating a very eerie kind of echo with multiple voices. During one rehearsal I had a student come and tell me he could achieve the same effect with his music software. I told him we were going to do it live, and he got frustrated with me. After the service on Good Friday when we lead people to the cross with nothing more than voices and candles, he came up to me and said, "Okay, I get it now."

Forget about Space Soldiers video games with vibrating controllers. How many students actually play at one time? What happens when you have a student who spends every waking moment in the land of Primus-Woot? (I just made that up. Don't go looking for it.) Play Hide and Seek. Play the Sardines version where once you find the hider you hide with them.

Physical contact.

Real spoken words.

These often go unappreciated until you don't have them for awhile.

**TIP #17: Turn off virtual and embrace actual.**

## 18

## Eminem, Not M&M's

For years now I have tried to use the music that my students are listening to and turn it into a Bible study. Yes, I once had to explain to a parent that we had Eminem in Sunday school and not M&Ms. (Thought we frequently have those too.)

For some reason, many churches feel the need to use "the Christian version" of popular artists. Why not just use the artists that students already have on their iPods?

I explained this to a fellow youth worker once, and he praised me for "subverting the culture." He said that what I was doing was "taking it back." That bothered for a long time. I wasn't subverting the culture. That would seem to indicate that something was wrong with the song or the video to begin with, and I was, somehow, making it okay with God.

All inspiration is God-breathed. If God breathes into Marshall Mathers and inspires him to write a profanity-laden rap, can we really say that it is less worthy than any of today's Christian bands? Simply because we (or maybe some parents) find those words objectionable? (Jesus was a carpenter. What do you think he said when he hit his thumb with a hammer?)

Find out what your students like to listen to. If you can't understand the lyrics, look them up online. What is the singer saying? What voices are in the song? Ask yourself, could this be a prayer? Could it be the words of someone in the Bible?

The psalms are not fluffy poetry recited by Shakespearean actors who strut and fret their hour upon the stage, and then are heard of no more. The psalms are punk lyrics, country music, and smoky New Orleans blues. To say that God is not present in a singer's music or the Holy Spirit would not inspire such "garbage" is to put a limit on God (which is not possible.)

If God is in all places and all time in all things in all people, who are we to say otherwise.

Use the music your students are already listening to. Let them hear the message in the lyrics. Eventually they will start hearing it themselves.

**TIP #18: If it's God breathed, who are we to try to suffocate it?**

**19**

# Youth Ministry Expands
# Beyond the Youth Room

Robert is a teenager. He's seventeen. His parents are divorced. His mother makes him go to youth meetings; his father doesn't see the point. Robert has a part-time job at a local ice cream place, he plays basketball, he has a girlfriend, and he's struggling to maintain at least a B average so he can get a scholarship next year when he graduates. If you're a youth minister you're lucky if you see Robert once every two months. Robert is a good kid who needs prayers and support and encouragement. That part of your job, however, isn't seen by the people who keep asking, "How many?"

A youth leader can have ten students in the youth room on Sunday, and only a few of them may be part of the ten that are there next week. Ask this: How many teens are in the program? or, How many teenagers does the youth minister have contact with on a weekly basis? Do we count conversations online? Yes! Do we count the friend who came with a regular student who will probably not come again because she attends her own church? Yes!

The number of students in the youth room will vary according to the sports seasons, what's on TV, what movies are coming out that weekend, Dad's work schedule, mom's car repair, whether Mom or Dad is angry with a sibling, home chores, homework, or the amount of sleep a student got the night before. The number of students who are eligible to be in the program is directly proportional to the *mood* of the parent!

**TIP #19: The success of a program cannot be measured by the number of students in the room on Sunday night.**

**20**

# Tell Stories

A Sunday school teacher I know told me she once planned a really great lesson on a batch of verses from proverbs. As she was about to teach, a student came in looking tired and weary and sporting a blackeye. Someone said, "What happened to you?"

He said, "Nuthin, I just got in a fight last night."

First of all, "Nuthin" and "I just got in a fight" is an oxymoron. Nevertheless, with that one word the student took control of the class and proceeded to tell the story for the next twenty minutes of exactly how "nuthin'" went down.

The Bible is full of laws and poetry and prophesies, but it is also filled with some of the most bizarre and wonderfully screwy stories ever told.

Start out a lesson by telling your students the story of a bald man who used the power of God to call forth two angry bears from the woods who mauled forty-two youths to death! (2 Kings 2:23–24).

Or maybe the story of a young man who wanted to marry the king's daughter, but the king hated the young man, and so as a "wedding gift" he demanded that the young suitor bring him the foreskins of one hundred Philistine soldiers. (Thinking that if you got close enough to people to cut off their foreskins, one of them was going to kill you.) Yet the young suitor prevailed.

Tell the story; don't read it. Speak it aloud in your car during the week so it sounds like a story you'd tell around the dinner table. You don't even have to mention that it's from the scriptures right away. Get them hooked then bring them in.

TIP #20: Kick off your lessons with some of the Bible's most bizarre tales, and you'll keep their attention longer than if you began with, "Let's open our lesson books and read aloud, shall we?"

# Don't Take Yourself Too Seriously

The whole idea that "you are the only Jesus some people will ever see" is a wonderful axiom, but don't take it too literally. God already sent one savior; you're the second string.

Too many times youth ministers will enter their careers armed with a guitar slung over their back, a giant box of markers under their arm, and a word-for-word memorization of the book of Leviticus. These will not matter a jot or a tittle if you can't match the champion Dew drinker belch for belch. I knew a guy who, on his first winter retreat at a new church, tried to outdo a young man in the pancake eating contest. The youth ate seventeen. The new youth worker ate fifteen and then all fifteen made, shall we say, a reappearance for Jesus.

Enter into a program, not as the savior and authority, but as a fellow traveler who just happens to be the one with the driver's license. You are on this road trip together. Every road trip has the joker, the girl who knows how to fold a map properly, the kid who brings the homemade brownies, and the person who knows the words to every song that comes on the radio.

Walking into the youth room as the hero who will straighten this all out: "Just come to *me* young people and I'll tell you the answers to everything!" That's going to earn you an empty youth room unless you have a box of Krispy Kreme with you.

**TIP #21: Learn to laugh at yourself. Nobody likes a know-it-all.**

**22**

# Open the Door to Healing

Many times parents will start "strongly encouraging" their off-spring to start attending a youth group meeting because the parents simply don't know how to handle this kid any more. Mike Yaconelli said, "Ever notice that when kids get hormones their parents get crazy?"

You may have a mom who has just "had it up to here!" with little Jennifer's antics and would gladly just drop her off at the church for a few hours of peace. However, her expectation is "Fix my kid." And we, the youth ministers, feel like failures because we didn't or simply couldn't do it. Jennifer still ends up in juvenile detention or pregnant or gets brought home by the police after driving drunk, or simply loses her cool on a daily basis and cusses Mom out. Sometimes you just can't.

What you can do is open the door.

You can show the teenager that life is good even if you are not fighting for it. You can teach them that the entire world is open to them if they simply look around. You can teach them that the way to a job that sucks less than the one they are in is to do the one they are in to the best of their ability.

One of the worst things to say to a teenager is "It's not the end of the world." Because to them, it is. Teenagers live fully in the moment. Everything is "now" to them. As a youth minister you can open their mind to the big picture:

Help them understand that actions have consequences, that studying now will help them get that scholarship next year, that getting home before curfew will help you get the curfew extended for next time.

But you cannot fix a kid who does not want to be fixed. You can open doors but you can't push them through.

Jesus did not sit in the boat with Peter and say, "Go." He stood out on the water and said, "Come."

**TIP #22: Sometimes the best you can do is encourage them to take a step out of the boat.**

# 23

# Youth Ministry Should Be a Sensory Experience

What does Bible study taste like? No, not the Oreos you picked up on the way in. Find the message you are trying to convey and provide a sensory application.

When Elijah is lying in the cave hiding out, an angel comes and bakes for him. King James tells us it was a cake or, in some translations, cakes. We also know that the cakes sustained him for many days. (Those must have been some amazing cakes.) So we're probably talking about homemade buttermilk biscuits here, or maybe some warm, fresh Kripsy Kreme donuts. Provide your students with a taste of Bible study.

Show them what "anointing oil" was made of. When David had the oil poured over his head, when Jesus had his feet anointed, what was that oil made of? What did it smell like? A little research shows us that you can make a least a reasonable facsimile with olive oil, cinnamon, and expensive perfume. A touch of Obsession mixed with pumpkin pie spice and some olive oil from the grocery store will give kids the idea. Let them touch it, smell it, even taste it. To have this rubbed on your feet or combed into your hair would have been the greatest compliment you could give a person in Jesus' time. To create this expensive tribute and then to use it only for one purpose shows just how important the receiver of this blessing was.

Dig out the Queen classic "We Will Rock You." How high does the volume go on the CD player in the youth room? (So what if the pastor's office is next door; this is for Jesus.) Let your kids feel the vibration beneath their feet and then talk about the triumphant entry into Jerusalem. Talk about how Jesus told the

Pharisees that even if the voice were silenced, the rocks would start to sing.

Try finding one powerful sense per lesson, and it will help the point stick like glue in your students' memories.

**TIP #23: We all have five senses. See if your lesson can use them all.**

**24**

# Try Something New
# Every Time

"A rut ain't nothin' but a grave with the ends dug out."

If I could tell you who first said that, I would, but I heard it from a minister who was speaking at a summer camp. It still happens to be very true.

Youth ministry is difficult because it must change in order to survive. Many jobs require us to find a groove, slide in, and then stay there and surf the current.

Imagine you are driving and you hold your hand out the window. Don't we all try and find that "sweet spot" where we can surf the wind as we cruise down the highway. Is that the goal of life in general? Find the path of least resistance and surf it.

Youth work is about holding your hand out flat and bracing it against the wind. Youth ministry can't be the same as it was in the last decade. It can't be the same as it was last year—or even yesterday.

Youth work requires us to live and teach in the moment.

The church loves tradition. If you had a successful pancake breakfast fund raiser last year, it's already on the books for next year.

Keep the youth and your church guessing. Keep everything new so that your students have no idea what to expect when they walk through the door. I knew a wonderful woman who was a retired high school art teacher. The first day of the school year she'd wear a black smock, clunky shoes, and black horn-rimmed glasses and she'd pull her hair into a tight bun. She would scold students for holding the pencil wrong and slouching. The next day she wore butterfly wings and insisted that the kids listen to music while they drew. In a matter of days every kid was guessing what crazy-ms-Cocheren was going to do next. No one hated to go to her class.

Constants are important. Your students should know they can always feel "safe" to be who they are in the youth room. They should know they can always talk to you about whatever is going on in their lives and know they won't be judged.

**TIP #24: Keep kids guessing, and they will keep coming back just to see what you come up with next.**

**25**

# Learn How to Fall

A few years ago my daughter came to an age when boys began calling my house. (A disturbing notion for any father.) I knew it was time for me either to purchase a firearm or enroll her in self-defense classes. We decided to take Aikido as father and daughter. The very first thing we learned was how to fall. We spent hours learning how to roll, both backward and forward, and return to our feet. This is the most basic instruction. We could learn nothing else until we learned this.

Not every meeting you plan is going to go well, not every event will bring in the teens, not every idea you have will be approved by the administrative board. We take our hits. We hit the ground. If we don't learn to roll with the failures, we will never be able to rise up and try again. Not everyone is going to be impressed by what we do. There are a few in every congregation who, it seems, will line up to take a shot at the youth minister. Like in Aikido we learn to get out of the way. We learn to absorb. We learn to fall and come back.

**TIP #25: Coming back from mistakes makes you stronger. Coming back quickly makes you a master.**

# 26

# Learn to Punt

The best laid plans of mice and men quite often go awry. Okay, let us rephrase for the youth minister shall we? Whatever can go wrong will go wrong. If you don't have a backup plan for your backup plan you could wind up being stuck someplace you don't want to be. When all else fails, be ready to punt. Go with the flow. Take the situation at hand and come up with the best solution for the moment and go with it. You have to be able to handle yourself in a crisis because crises will come up. If the kid who promised to bring brownies shows up and says "Whoops. Was that for today?" You should probably have a stash of Ding Dongs in your closet. Your lesson on the book of Jeremiah can wait if a student at the high school was killed in a drunk-driving accident in the middle of the week. Sometimes this is as easy as opening yourself up to the Holy Spirit and seeing where it takes you. Sometimes it means having a place nearby where you can go get ice cream.

**TIP #26: When the wave comes your way, you better know how to surf.**

## 27

# Expect Miracles

I have a friend who is an Episcopal priest. Her name is Madge. One of her favorite phrases is "Miracles happen, when you're Madge."

It seems to be true.

The Reverend Doctor Marjorie, as "normal" people call her, firmly believes that miracles were happen to her—all the time.

Rev. Madge believes that something amazing and wonderful will happen when she walks down the street and quite often, it does. There is a story about her taking her youth group down the street from the church to a coffee shop. It was group of about ten teenagers. Fully believing that something amazing and wonderful could happen at any moment, Rev Madge took a short cut through an alley and found a dumpster with two sets of feet sticking out of the top. They were bare feet, bare *plastic* feet. Someone had thrown away two full-sized mannequins. Madge, being Madge, crawled into the dumpster to retrieve them. One she gave away and other was given the name Roxy and traveled with the youth group on mission excursions and field trips and more than once found her way into a worship service.

I'll give you a moment to picture what it would be like for the senior pastor to look up from the pulpit to the balcony of the church and seeing fifteen or more teens grinning from ear to ear and one young woman in the middle of the group who seemed—a little stiff.

Attitude is everything. If you go into meeting thinking this is never going to work, guess what could happen? Many of us pray for rain during a drought, but how many of us take an umbrella to church? If you think, "The board will never approve this idea, what's the most likely outcome?"

If we go into a mission project fully believing that something amazing and wonderful will happen, it will.

If we treat every moment we spend with our youth as a chance for the love of God to work in amazing and unexpected ways, guess what can happen?

**TIP #27: Miraculous things will happen if we believe they will.**

# 28

# You Are the Message

Songwriter Baz Lurhmann said in his wonderful song "Sunscreen." Remember the compliments your receive. Forget the insults. If you figure out how to do this, tell me how."

Teenagers are bombarded with messages that say, "You're not pretty unless you are wearing *this*." "You're not a real man unless you have done *that*." You're not worthy of my attention until you . . ."

Sometimes these messages can be found in church. We hold the heroes of the Bible up on high and say, "Be like Moses; he was obedient." Or "Be like David, he was a good and righteous man." Or "We must strive every day to be more like Jesus. Then God will love you and your problems will go away."

If you can figure out how to do this, tell me how.

Moses tried to get out of the job five times. David had a tendency to spy on his neighbors when they were bathing, to dance almost naked in parades, and occasionally to kill people. For the record, Jesus was also human (in addition to being God-incarnate). Jesus had bad breath and BO. He got tired and cranky. He had moments of doubt and pain.

We cannot hold ourselves up as solutions or models of perfect behavior. "I found Jesus and now my problems are over." It isn't true.

**TIP #28: Students are much more likely to listen to you if you approach them, not as the one with the food, but as one beggar showing another beggar where the food is.**

# 29

# You Are Not Too Old

Question: How does a teenager count?

Answer: 17 . . . 18 . . . 19 . . . old . . . dead.

If you are twenty-one your and leading a junior high youth group, the already sees you as old.

Dumb question to ask youth: "Well, how old do you think I am?" This never ends well.

So the question is, When is too old to be doing youth ministry? Answer: Check your pulse. Got one? Then you are not too old. You might *feel* too old to be doing youth ministry on the third day of the mission trip, but you are not.

I've already mention a woman named Sally who volunteered to chaperone her first youth mission trip when she was sixty-eight! She was a retired teacher and missed working with young people. Did she haul buckets of paint? No. Did she climb on the roof and repair shingles? No. But she could cook, she could paint, she could scrape, she could listen to kids who were tired and complaining or were full of questions about poverty and sickness. She could pray.

Let's put this is geek terms.

Maybe you are not Luke Skywaker anymore. Maybe you can't do seven roller coasters in an hour or eat the hot pepper sauce on your taco. Maybe you can't play kick-ball like you once did or help move the furniture to one end of the room so the group can play Shuffle Your Buns. Maybe you can't make the Castle run in twelve parsecs. (Was that too geek?)

Perhaps you can't be Skywalker, but you can be Qui Gon Jin. You can be the teacher. You can be the mentor and allow someone else to do the heavy lifting once in awhile.

You can be Luke Skywalker. You can swing over chasms, pull out the blaster and fire randomly, and jump into adventure with an enthusiasm only someone new to the game can possess.

You can be Obi-Wan Kenobi. You can pursue adventure with the perspective of someone who's done it before. You can give the "Lukes" of this world guidance and protection. With a simple phrase you can disarm guards, calm a situation, and strike a bargain when you need a spaceship (or at least a fifteen-passenger van). Having "been there and done that" gives you the responsibility of guiding those who have never done it before.

In addition to the Luke Skywalkers and Obi-Wan Kenobis, there are a few Yodas in youth ministry. Not many, but a few. Yoda did a lot of observing. He offered advice and tutelage. He knew the right time to speak and the right thing to say. Moreover, when no one else believed that miracles were possible, Yoda lifted the X-wing fighter out of the swamp.

**TIP #29: With age comes wisdom. With wisdom comes knowing when to invest in a better air mattress.**

# 30

## Everyone Is Safe Here

There is no such thing as a practical joke in youth ministry. There is no place for humor that makes a student the butt of any kind of joke. Even if you think the student can handle it, you don't always know what's going on inside the kid's head.

On a winter retreat I led as a newbie youth minister, a group of guys decided it would be funny to raid the girls' cabin and swipe their underwear. Every guy showed up for dinner wearing a pair of panties as a hat. The girls all thought it was embarrassing, but they all laughed. All but one. A boy on whom she had a severe crush came to the table wearing her wonder woman girl-briefs on his head like a crown. He made one or two rude comments, and then the boys all gave the underwear back to the counselor, who acted as though it was just a matter of boys-will-be-boys.

It was the last time the young lady came to a youth event or meeting. No amount of joshing, cajoling, or encouraging words would remove that scar of embarrassment from her memory.

Youth meetings are safe places. Youth rooms are sanctuaries. (Not like in the big room with the stained-glass windows but like in a hunchback screaming, "Sanctuary!") When teenagers show up to at a youth meeting, they should know they will not be picked on, laughed at, or bullied, not by other students and not by the youth leaders.

Sometimes the youth room becomes "the only place I can be myself." It is the respite from the rest of the week. It is two hours away from Mom and Dad's constant screaming, coach's belittling, and the bullies around the corner waiting to see if they can send you splaying books all over the floor. Jesus called the church to be the place where all are loved and accepted, no matter who they are.

Don't put up with those who laugh at others in a youth meeting. Don't put up with insults and sexist or bigoted comments. Stop them early. Let everyone know: this is where you are safe. Sometimes you find out that those who were doing the picking or bullying needed that place too.

**TIP #30: Youth group meetings are the place where you can be exactly who God made you to be.**

# It's About Opening Doors

There's an old saying that goes "You can say things while doing the dishes that you can't say at the dinner table."

There is a safety in keeping someone busy. Sometimes a face-to-face conversation is too blunt or too "in your face." You can have a conversation about anything when someone's hands are busy. I know a youth worker who keeps a big jar of "bendy" toys on her desk. It's great way to keep someone's hands busy and opens up the opportunity for conversation.

Many of my junior high students could not sit in a circle and talk about the evening's topic. However, if I have a game like Apples to Apples or even a simple card game I can ask all the same questions and it is a lot less threatening.

Always keep the door open for discussion. If a topic comes up that your students seem to want to talk about while you are on your way to the point you were trying to make, a detour is not out of the way. See where it goes. See what doors open up for you to ask a question.

Many students don't want to express an opinion or open themselves up in front of others. You may get emails after a meeting from students who have been thinking about the meeting during the past week. Some of the best conversations I've had with students have been after the day is done on the mission trip or the lock-in, and a student says, "Can I talk to you for a second?" Don't let this opportunity get away simply because the meeting is over.

**TIP #31: Question Time or Discussion Time should be all the time.**

## 32

# There's Something to Be Said for a Cheap Laugh

There is nothing wrong with a cheap laugh.

I was on a winter retreat a few years ago. We were staying in a small lodge in northeast Ohio. It was cold, we'd spent the day sled riding (and talking about Jesus of course). That evening the caretaker stopped by to tell us that the case or two of cheap (I mean *cheap*) diet root beer was left by the previous group and we were more than welcome to drink it.

A few hours later one of my students, shall we say, "witnessed" the love of Jesus to the group with a noise that defied description. It came from his toes. I was going to comment on the sheer inappropriateness of that sort of behavior on a church outing. Instead I decided to see if I could top him. I did. The students then swarmed on the cases of wretched soda, and what followed was a contest the likes of which had never before been seen or heard. A girl named Bonnie brought forth something that was demonic in nature. One of my seniors began the alphabet and made it all the way to the letter "I," which came out like "EYEEEEEEEEEEEE".

We were laughing so hard we all had tears in our eyes. (I'm honestly starting to break myself up as I write about it.) My fellow chaperone was lying on the floor unable to get her breath. Even my most prissy girls joined in.

It was a good ten minutes of pure joy, unadulterated laughter, a complete and total abandonment to the moment. The walls came down and we all giggled our way through the rest of the night.

Is it crude to write about this in a book about igniting your ministry? (Yes, I am aware there is an ignition joke there, but if you thought of it then I don't have to make it.) It probably is inappropriate but it's absolutely real. It's honest. It happens. It is a moment that I still think about and remember as a moment of change in that group. Laughing together brings us together.

You cannot tell me that in "Bible times" Jesus and twelve guys wandered around the country together for three years and not one time did a contest break out? Are you kidding? These were *guys*. They were fishermen and tax collectors and at least one carpenter. They were human beings and I would assume all of them were subject to the normal functions of the human body. Why does it bother some people to think of Jesus as having bad breath or BO or boogers? Making Jesus human for your students can actually bring them closer to him whereas putting Jesus up on a pedestal in his clean white robe can, in some ways, drive them further away.

Should you make the "contest" part of your weekly meetings? Probably not, but when moments like that arise in all their spontaneous glory, it's okay to let it happen rather than shake the finger of shame.

**TIP #32: Jesus was also human. So are you. So are your teenagers. Celebrate human-ness.**

# 33

# There Is No Such Thing as an Inactive Member

Let me tell you about Chris (not his real name) You probably have a "Chris" in your group.

Chris's parents are divorced. His mother insists he be a part of the youth group, while his dad relishes every moment of the weekends he gets with Chris so he does not take him to church on Sundays. Chris is also on the basketball team. Chris has a girlfriend and a part-time job. He maintains a 3.6 grade average and is working hard to bring it up so he can receive a tuition break when he goes to college.

I'm lucky if I see Chris at a meeting once a month.

How many of your students' attendance is based on something other than their own desire to show up? I once worked (briefly) for a church that used meeting and fund-raiser attendance to determine a student's fee to go on the mission trip. Is that fair? How can we reward or punish students based on the Sunday night mood of Mom and Dad, or the amount of homework given by this year's mean teacher, or the supervisor who calls at the last minute and says, "Somebody is sick, can you come work today?"

If you have a Chris in your group, you should be dancing on the table every time he walks through the door. "WHOOO HOOOO. You're here!"

It's the Chris's in our groups that depend on the emails, the Facebook quotes, the daily texts. Sporadic attendance is now the norm. You many have the same number of students week to week at your meetings but sometimes they might not be the same students.

Communication is vital in all its forms. No student should ever think, "I guess I'm not a real member of the group." Youth leaders must make sure they have updated emails, phone numbers, and Web pages for all their students. The Sunday night meeting as we know it will soon be a thing of the past. It will always be a part of youth ministry, but how much longer can it be the focal point? You can have members of your group who can't show for months at a time, yet we must see them as vital and active members just the same.

**TIP #33: You don't have to show up to be in the group. You can be part of the group without having to be physically present.**

**(34)**

# The Joy of Texting

True Story: It was two o'clock in the morning. My cell phone was next to my bed. It chirped its you-have-a-text greeting. I picked it up and it said, "But I still love him."

One of my girl students had been texting a friend in the middle of the night. She had broken up with her boyfriend and was commiserating with another girl from her school. She didn't mean to send me the text, but apparently our names are close on her list. I texted her back and asked what was going on. I wound up spending the next hour on my couch in the middle of the night texting back and forth with a teenager whose world was ending because her boyfriend dumped her.

I'm collecting a list of "stupid things adults say to teenagers". One of the top ten will be "It's not the end of the world." Teens live in the moment. For that girl, it absolutely was the end of the world. It was the worst night of her life, and I got to be there for it. She didn't want to call or send an email or talk about it on Sunday. It was that moment she had to get through. Suddenly the unlimited texting feature on my phone is the most important youth ministry tool I have.

I was the last person I knew to get a cell phone. But I finally realized that I was becoming the deterrent to communication by my refusal to get with the times. Events like the one above were a conversion for me. Stay up to date on what's out there. By the time you read this there will be new technologies that are not available as I write. Know what your students are using to connect with each other. Use it to connect with them; eventually you will find a way to use it to help them connect with God.

**TIP #34: lrn 2 rd txtng (It's a lot like Hebrew)**

# 35

# Let Them Be Themselves

When I was in high school, I knew a kid named David. We called him Dave, and his parents called him Davy. Watching him go in and out of his house was like watching a science fiction movie. That front door was, let's say, a Transmogrifier. Is that a cool science fiction word? When he walked in the front door he became Davy; when he walked back out he became Dave. Inside his house he was everything his parents wanted him to be. (He was hiding much from them.) Pleasing them and being the kind of son they wanted was his obsession. A group of us could sit in the car in his driveway and watch his entire body language change when he came outside. With us, he was just Dave.

Your students are bombarded with everyone else's idea of what they should be. As youth ministers we can say, "Just be yourself" all we want, but that doesn't always work; that message doesn't always get through. High school can be a hard place and sometimes you have to just survive.

Let them be who they are. Encourage them to follow their dreams but let them see the future as unknown. You will have students who truly know what they want to do as a career and others who have no clue. Help them find their gifts. Encourage them to use them.

If you were to talk to any adult and say, "When was the most confusing and bewildering time in your life?" Most would say, "When I was sixteen or seventeen or thereabouts." A huge percentage of adults will agree that the teen years are the most frustrating. Yet this is when we go to teenagers and say "Well, what do you want to do with the *rest of your life*?" The "rest of your life" is a long time. It's unfair to ask that question, yet many schools give tests to see what you should do. We give them Myers-Briggs tests and say, "Really? A doctor? Oh, I don't think so." Some high schools ask students to pick an "area of concentration."

Students get confused messages: "Why don't you just grow up and accept some responsibility?" along with "Why are in you such a hurry? Slow down. Enjoy life."

Encourage students to be who they are, to right here and right now be the best they can be. Once they begin to work on themselves, it's amazing how many doors begin to open in front of them.

**TIP #35: Build your students from the inside out.**

# 36

## Respect the Sexton

One of the most contentious relationships youth ministers have is with the church sexton. Do you know that word? As a rule, ask your students to stop using the word "janitor" or "custodian." Sexton is a very old word for the person who was employed to care for the church. Very often the sexton-lived on the premises. They rang the bell in the morning. They dug the graves for funerals. They were part of the building.

How do you respect a sexton? Here are a few ideas:

Bring your group to the church on a Saturday morning. Break out lots of Windex and paper towels and don't stop until ever window in the building has been cleaned, especially those around the doors. Then ask the students to come back and stand near the doors on Sunday morning and watch how many people put their hands on the clean glass. (They aren't allowed to say anything to the members—just watch.) Explain that this is what the sexton goes through every day.

Every sexton in every church has a list of projects they hope they can get to "one of these days." Ask your sexton to choose something off the list and give it to the youth.

How often does your sexton work on Christmas eve? Are they the last one out the door after everyone else has gone home? Decide in advance that the youth will bring supper for the sexton on that night.

An occasional pint of Ben & Jerry's in the freezer with the sexton's name on it doesn't hurt either.

Your sexton can be your best advocate or your biggest detractor. Your sexton knows all the places where two kids could hide during a lock-in. They can defend you when the kitchen is messy. They quietly let you know if one of your students broke into the fellowship time cookies).

Caring for God's house is different from caring for an office building. Everyone is a minister. Everything speaks. When the clear light of day breaks through the stained-glass windows, people want to (mentally) hear the choirs of angels singing. They don't want to see cobwebs or dust.

And if you think *you* have critics, imagine what it's like to be the sexton. People leave snotty Kleenex in the pews, half empty coffee cups on the window sills, and you don't want to know what get's left in the restrooms.

**TIP #36: The sexton is an important relationship in your ministry. It's important that respect be mutual.**

**37**

# Get Out of the Building

It's been said that the three most important things to remember when buying a house or starting a business are (1) Location, (2) Location, and (3) Location.

Get out of the building. If you are going to have a lesson about the night that Jesus was born, hold the meeting behind a local hotel near the dumpster. (How often do we see pictures of a clean stable filled with clean straw, as if that smelled pretty.) This lesson is much cooler if you walk your kids to the hotel, (park down the street), arrange with the manager ahead of time, and have the clerk say "Sorry, there is no room in the inn."

If your lesson is Peter walking on water, who in your church has a pool?

If you are teaching about Jesus calling the fishermen, can you hold the lesson on a beach? On a boat?

Take your group to a local airport or hospital that has a chapel. Pray there.

Every kid has a digital camera built into their phone. Isn't the mall a wonderful place for a scavenger hunt?

If you have one of those nights where only three kids show up, sounds like a Starbucks run to me.

The underlying lesson here (besides being able to talk your way out of trouble with a security guard) is that "church" is a verb. Church happens. Whenever two or three of you are gathered (that sounds familiar doesn't it?) *that* is church. Church is what we do, not where we meet.

**TIP #37: Remember you are a youth group, not necessarily a church group. Don't be afraid to take your students out of the building**

# Pray

Does prayer seem like a given? Sometimes the only prayer you hear at a youth meeting is "Rub a dub dub. Thanks for the grub. Yeaaaaaaa, GOD!"

(I wonder if God gets tired of that one.)

Many teens have not been taught to pray, outside of meals and bedtime prayers. We give them the same prayers they are comfortable with, but we don't teach them that prayer works.

Pray every meeting. Pray for those who are there and those who aren't. Know when finals are so you can email prayers to your students.

Know who is sick in your congregation and lift them up in prayer. Create a set of postcards that say, "We prayed for you today." Have your students sign them and send them to every single member of your congregation. Don't be afraid to say, "I prayed for you today" to a student.

Take one meeting and hand out newspapers to your group. Have them find someone who needs prayers. Then have them dip their fingers in paint and cover over that article. Hang these sheets on the wall.

Prayer does not have to be the hands folded quietly in front of you prayer. (Who decided that? Who decided that hands folded in front of you was praying. What if they had decided sticking your finger in your ear was a prayer position?)

Stand in a circle shoulder to shoulder. Now have everyone put their right hand into the circle with their right thumb extended to the left. Ask each person to grab the thumb of the person next to them while allowing their own thumb to be grabbed by the person to their left. There, you have a tightly woven prayer circle Sit with your students in church. Pass notes and generally see if you can make them giggle, but be serious when it comes to prayer. Take them in the sanctuary and light a candle and pray together or take them out in the pouring rain and pray with your arms outstretched. Prayer is too big to be reduced to something that sounds like a nursery rhyme.

**TIP #38: Show your students how important prayer is. Model it for them. They will turn to it when they need it most.**

**(39)**

# Recognize Other Religions' Holidays

When was the last time you celebrated Yom Kippur? Okay, when was the last time you looked up Yom Kippur?

What if there is one God up there doing thousands of things to get our attention? The Internet is a wonderful tool. Use it to see what the high holy days of other religions are during the year. See if you can get a basic idea of what these are. It's not easy. Have you ever tried to explain the Christmas story to an adult who has never heard it?

Celebrate Ramadan with your students. Have a Seder meal. Understand what Chanukah is. (No, Timmy it's not Jewish Christmas)

There is a wide range of celebrations out there, and all of them are designed to bring individuals closer to God. Find out what prayers are written for these days. What foods are served and why?

Take a look at this list: Right Understanding. Right purpose. Right speech. Right conduct. Right livelihood. Right effort. Right alertness. Right concentration.

See anything anti-Christian there? See anything that you think God would have a problem with? Probably not. But if you told your students you would be teaching the Eightfold path from the Four Nobel truths of Buddha, do you think you might get their attention? (At least from their parents you would.)

I highly recommend books like *The Complete Idiot's Guide to World Religions*. You can pick up "the least you need to know" about other religions' ideas of God.

**TIP #39: We aren't all in the same boat, but we are all on the same journey.**

**40**

# Protect the Questions

One of the great truths about Christianity is that it's a mystery. This is a problem with many teenagers because they want black-and-white answers. When life is confusing, it's so much easier to have someone give you the answers. Youth ministry (all ministry really) is about protecting the questions.

Why did God allow those planes to fly into the buildings on September 11?

Answer: "I really don't know."

Why didn't God stop Grandma's cancer?

Answer: "I really don't know."

Why did God stick me with this face?

Answer: "I really don't know."

That kind of sucks doesn't it?

Answer: Yes, it does.

The problem with God's will is that it isn't a "To Do" list. There's no list of "do this and God will love you." God will love us anyway. Figuring out what God wants is like translating the instructions of Monopoly into a language you've never spoken.

As I write this section of the book, just to the right side of my screen there is an open "Thesaurus window." I looked up the word "confusing." The program gave me this list: puzzling, perplexing, baffling, mystifying, bewildering, and then as an antonym: clear.

How boring is the word "clear" compared with "mystifying." God does not cause bad things to happen. Bad things happen. That's why God gave us each other.

I once heard a Sunday school teacher say, "God made the rose and Satan made the thorn." The fact is that God made the rose and the thorn. God made the sun that shines on the rose and made the bee that buzzes around it, and God made the tailor who made the jacket with the buttonhole where someone put the rose on the man as he waited for his bride to walk down the aisle. God put that plan together.

God did not give grandma cancer.

God did not send a hurricane to central Florida because Disney offered benefits to same-sex partners.

The twenty-eighth verse of the eighth chapter of Romans says that God takes all things and makes them work together. All things. God and bad.

Eventually you will have to deal with the hard questions from your students. Most of them will start with "Why would God . . ."

The answer is going to be "I don't know."

Ever go to a movie for a second or third time? It's different isn't it? If you know what's going to happen you might start to listen to the music or acknowledge the actor, or critique the script or warn the person next to you, "Oh, this is a cool part. Watch this." However, you aren't part of the story, are you? You aren't sucked in the way you were the first time. So it is with the hard questions.

Teach your students that to know the answer to, "Why, God, why?" is to cease to be part of the story.

The question "Why?" opens up a brand new door for your ministry.

The truth is that anyone who tells you they have all the answers is either lying or selling something. You don't have all the answers but you can gain more respect and points with your youth when you say "I don't know what I think about that either so let's work it out together." Our job as ministers is to protect the questions. Let there be a mystery to faith. Let there be a sense of wonder and searching. You should be asking more questions, not answering the ones in front of you. Belief is nothing if you don't know what you believe in.

We have to be able to teach kids that faith is stepping out of the boat whether you have all the answers or not. Even the disciples didn't get it all the time. Jesus was constantly saying, "You still don't get, it do you?" Even at the resurrection Matthew 28 says "they worshiped him but some doubted". You can have questions and still be Christian. You can have doubts and still be Christian. If complete and total faith were the requirement for church membership, there would be no churches.

**TIP: #40: The answer is, "I don't know. Let's talk about it."**

**41**

# Use Your Gifts

God is God. God is always present. The idea of "invoking" the spirit of God seems somehow irrelevant to me. It's not about "invoking"; instead lets think of it as "connecting." One of the beauties of a connecting theology is that everyone can do it differently.

Look at the disciples. Jesus called tax collectors and fishermen, men who worked with their hands and men who worked with their minds.

I'm not a sports person; I never have been. There are organizations like the Fellowship of Christian Athletes that do wonderful work connecting teens to God through sports. I've never had a softball team as part of my ministry.

My gift is words. I can write. I can create liturgy, tell stories, and write letters. I have a former student who as of this writing is in seminary to become a youth minister. I just know she's going to show up to her first youth meeting someday with an easel pad and a giant box of Crayola markers under her arm.

That is the gift she brings. That is how she will teach. My friend and fellow youth worker Al has a much more athletic program. Organizing giant dodge ball events is how he ministers.

Every youth minister will bring their own gifts to the table. It is one of the primary lessons we teach. What are your gifts and how are you going to use them for God?

I believe this is how we say, "thank you," to God for the gifts he has given us: we use them.

When a new youth minister comes into a church, the dynamic of the group and the leaders will change. No youth minister is going to come into an existing program and make it work like the youth minister before them. Everyone brings different gifts to the table.

You might lose some group members. It happens. If the new youth minister is a fan of sacred dance, then the athletes might go find another group. (*Pause for gasping.*) This is okay. Churches often freak out when they see numbers dwindling after a new youth minister begins.

I know a girl who was "Goth" before there was Goth. She grew up on Joan Jett and tough girl rockers. She ministered to the fringe kids, those who sat at the back of the room and didn't participate much. When she took on a new church to serve, the fringe kids (metaphorically) moved to the front of the room. A group that had once been populated by those who sat at the cool kids table shrunk from about fifty to fifteen, and the church seriously began to reconsider their decision to hire her. But the parents of the kids on the edge won out. The group grew slightly, not up to the original numbers, but the ministry itself became more active. Missions became a huge part of the group dynamic. Attendance at the Wednesday night Bible study doubled.

There is no "model" for youth ministry, or youth ministers for that matter. Every youth minister has a different set of gifts they bring to God's table.

**TIP #41: Groups will change and flow, and churches must learn to make room for whatever the next incarnation of the youth group becomes.**

# Rotate

Years ago I worked as a camp counselor at a church camp in Northeast Ohio. Every night after supper there was a certain amount of free time during which campers had a variety of activities open to them. One week the volleyball court seemed especially popular. Teams were formed, impromptu tournaments were created, and somewhere along the way it just got a little mean. Things were yelled across the net. Scoring had to be done by spiking the ball at the weakest players and then taunting them. Winning wasn't winning unless it was a blowout. Campers talked about the love of Jesus during the day, and then said vile things to each other on the court, even to their own teammates.

A few of the counselors developed a new system. After you served the ball, instead of rotating to the front of the line, you rotated to the *other team*. Many of the students protested (well, the ones on the winning team protested), but the counselors held firm. This was the new rule. It took a few days but eventually the idea of "there are no teams" sunk in. The goal of playing the game was not winning; it was playing the game. It was difficult for some campers to accept. There *had* to be winners and losers. That was how you played! This opened up new doors of discussion in evening groups.

Okay, so maybe you don't have a huge camp full of students. What would happen if you played musical chairs in your group and nobody was ever "out"? Take away a chair each round, of course, but never remove a player. When the music stops, everybody sits even if it means sitting on another player.

Here's another idea. Set up all the different board games you can find in your church's supply closet. Everything from Connect Four to Candyland to Monopoly. Break students into small groups, and have them start playing. When the whistle blows, everyone gets up and finds a new game to join.

Think of how the dynamic of a group would change if no one ever loses a game. The goal of the game is not to win, but to have fun playing.

There are two books that are out of print but can be found online: *The New Games Book* and *More New Games*. These are loaded with noncompetitive games designed simply to have fun. There are web sites where you can find these games.

All these go back to the idea of creating a place where everyone is welcome, everyone is accepted, everyone plays, and nobody sits on the sideline.

**TIP #42: Everyone plays on God's court.**

**43**

# Affirmation Builds Inner Strength

Adolescence is hard. Those who think it's not don't remember it. When was the last time one of your parents looked at their student and said, "You are so cool"?

If you want to build your group, build the individual students. Create wonderful and amazing individuals and you will have a wonderful and amazing group that does wonderful and amazing things.

Students are bombarded with negative messages in their lives (sometimes these come from the people who should most be in their corner.) Let Sunday Night Youth Meetings (or whenever you meet) become the place of affirmation. This involves a change in behavior on the youth leader's part.

Sometimes the change is subtle. You might be in a room with seven students and say aloud. "Gee where is everybody?" (yes, we've all done that one). How does that make the seven students feel who showed up?

Every time a student walks through the door the youth leaders should be overjoyed to see them. Every meeting should include affirmations for each student. Our lessons are often about becoming better people, doing what God wants to make the world better.

What about acknowledging how they are making the world better simply by being *in it*? Recognize that their presence makes the church better and makes you, the youth leader, happy to simply have them in the room.

Just a slight adjustment can make all the difference. Instead of texting, "GOOD LUCK ON THE FINAL" try saying, "YOU ARE SO

GONNA ROCK THIS FINAL" One opens the door for thoughts of mistakes and failure, the other assumes success.

Is this going to change someone's life? Actually, it can. You may be the only positive voice kids hear. Teenagers live in the "now." If what they hear is, "Man, this final is going *suck*." That's where they live. If the last voice they hear is "You so rock." Then they can live in that moment.

Bombard your students with positive messages and they will return to you. Youth meetings will be the place where they know they are not only loved and accepted, but celebrated.

This sounds like manipulation, but don't tell your students you are affirming them. Just do it. One of those "stupid things adults say to teenagers" is "I'm going to talk to you like you are an adult now." Why is that so bad? Because that means the rest of the time you think they are children. Don't tell your teens you are going to talk to them like an adult. Simply talk to them as if they are an adult.

The same works for affirmations.

**TIP #43: Constantly be a positive voice in your student's lives because too often you'll be the only one.**

# Teach Your Group to Affirm Others

Explain to your group that you want part of their "identity" as a group to be one that affirms others. Create traditions that they can participate in even outside the group.

It's the summer time and the neighborhoods will be filled with little kids and lemonade stands. The next time you're out driving around with your group and spot one of these future-Donald Trumps, pull over and unload everyone for a glass of weak Kool-Aid. Make sure your students play up the thirst-quenching goodness of the product and then *way* overtip the chef. It will make your group feel great and make a little kid's day. Make it a regular practice on youth outings, and soon your students will be doing it on their own with their friends in the car.

Many fast food places now have 99 cent menus or at the most $1.99 for a burger, fries, and a drink. Have every kid bring six bucks (tell them they can skip a movie for one weekend). Order as many meals as you can and then have your kids pass these out to the car that is last in line at the drive-through. Don't even say you're a church unless the driver asks. Just do it as a fun donation.

**TIP #44: The best way to cheer yourself up is to cheer someone else up (Mark Twain).**

# 45

## Never Minister
## Out of Money or Memory

Nothing can destroy a great idea like someone saying,"We've never done it that way before." Or "We'll never be able to afford that."

When working with your team of volunteer leaders or with your students, never accept either of those statements during a brainstorming session.

I have a friend named McNair who once worked for Walt Disney World and now teaches creative thinking (see online *www.mcnairwilson.com*). When he worked for the mouse there were certain meetings whose only purpose was ideas. Blue Sky meetings, he called them. No critical thinking involved. Just "What can we do?"

You can't start off with "What can we do that we can afford?" or "What can we do that the administrative board will let us get away with," or "What did we do in the past that seemed to work."

I tried planning a worship service for my students one time, and my team of adult leaders were shooting down each other's ideas left and right. So I said, "No more. Only positive thinking. What would we do if we had absolutely no restrictions whatsoever?" One of them suggested, "We could have Jesus show up."

Everyone laughed. But in the silence of the next moment we started to think, "How can we make that happen."

Eventually I found a college student with long hair and a beard who was willing to work for a T-shirt and a pizza. We put him in my senior pastor's white robe. We found a cheap fog machine. Then during a worship service about the disciples gathering together after the crucifixion—in the middle of listening to Don Francisco's "He Is Alive," Jesus walked into the room in a cloud of smoke. We told him not to speak but to touch each kid on the head and then walk back out.

(Note: If you are going to hire someone to be Jesus make sure they take out the earring. I heard about that one for years.)

Once we jettisoned the notion of "what we can afford" and "what was done in the past," we were able to create a worship experience that students still remind me of nearly fifteen years later.

**TIP #45: Don't be bogged down by memory or money. Let your imagination take you where you want to go and only then figure out a way to make it happen.**

# 46

# Celebrate the Temporary

Churches love permanence. If it worked once then it should work forever, right? They are afraid to change in fear of hurting someone's feelings. My grandmother donated that stove in 1976; you can't just throw it away!

I once worked for a church that had a mural of Noah's Ark on the wall in the nursery. Members of the administrative board could remember being children in that room and seeing that ark. It was discovered that the paint used in the mural was lead based at a time when lead-based paint was not a concern. The amount of time and energy spent trying save, restore, keep, or rescue that painting was staggering. People wept openly when it was decided to cover it and paint a new mural.

The youth of the church simply looked at these adults and thought "Really?"

We've said before that being young is to live in the now. One of the most dangerous things you can do as a group is to start a tradition that you can't back out of. I worked for a church where the students who painted the youth room all dipped their hands in paint and then left a print on the wall. The next year a new group added to the hand prints. When there was no room it was suggested that the wall be painted so a new generation could start over. Again, weeping. Not so much from the youth but from those who had gone on to college and had gotten wind that their beloved wall might be covered.

Tributes should be temporary. You can hang a giant cloth on the wall and let your seniors decorate it. Then cut it up and frame small squares as graduation gifts. Then start again. Your youth room should constantly be in a state of flux—never the same. New posters, new artwork should be the norm.

Teens are better at "been there done that" than adults are. Teenagers love what is new. So give it to them. When change is part of the group dynamic, you'll have fewer hurt feelings when it happens.

**TIP #46: Change is good.**

**47**

# Get Up and Move

Teenagers spend a better part of their day at a desk in a room for forty minutes at a pop. When you are fifteen and have enough energy bottled up to run a small city, this forty minutes is an eternity. When they get to youth meetings, do we really want to make them sit at a table and fill out reproducible sheets?

Get them up and moving whenever possible.

Take the words "FULL CONTACT" and put them in front of any board game in the Sunday school supply closet. What if you set up the Trivial Pursuit board outside? The game piece is now a pie pan. Players must rush to the square without being tackled and then answer the geography question.

When asking discussion questions, label the couches in your youth room TRUE and FALSE or A, B, C, and D.

Ask a question: "Is there such a thing as a literal hell?" Then say "Go." Let students pile on the couch that best fits their opinion and then have the discussion. Take your ordinary meeting and see how many ways you can make your students move. No, you can't burn the energy off with a game of dodge ball. Youth meetings should look like dance.

**TIP #47: Everyone should leave a youth meeting exhausted (not just the youth leader).**

# 48

## Acknowledge the Presence of God in All Things

God is here. Make sure your group is constantly aware of that concept; not so they don't swear or behave more like good little Christians, but so they know they are not alone. Be sure every meeting includes prayer. Pray for the spirit to guide them as they leave and ask God to be with them.

However, what if we need God to be a little more physical.

Teenagers need to see it, taste it, touch it, smell it, and see it.

Use icons. T-shirts and hats are fine but how many of them actually get worn outside of church or church activities.

One year, instead of the traditional mission trip T-shirt, I had dog-tags printed with the group name and our theme verse. (Thank God for *www.orientaltradingco.com*.) These get worn way more than a T-shirt. When I visit a kid's house I will almost always see it hanging somewhere.

Find a member of your church who likes to build things, or visit a local craft store for small wooden crosses. Paint these for one meeting, and then hand them out during future discussions—just as a physical item to hold in their hand when they speak.

When preparing a lesson ask, "What does this scripture passage smell like?" Caves, flowers, olive oil, peppermint lifesavers? (I once asked the question of my students "What do you think angels smell like?" One girl said, "Clean sheets and wedding cake frosting."

I haven't been able to get that image out of my mind and think of it every time I read about angels.

I once found a St. Christopher medal at a flea market. It was made of copper but the face of the saint had been rubbed off. Someone had spent a lot of time rubbing the medal as they prayed.

Don't shy away from tacky dashboard statues or joke Jesus action figures. See online *http://www.mcphee.com/shop/search. php?search_query=jesu.*

Whether created for a laugh for seriousness, there is something to be said for holding the physical form of a cross, Jesus, or God in your hand while you pray.

**TIP #48: Teenagers are physical beings. Let them use their senses when they pray.**

# ㊾

# Worship

Here's the magic word. Ready? *Ecclesia (Ek-Lay-SEE-ya)*.

It's Greek. It means a gathering of people for a specific purpose. It's not the same thing as "church." Church should be a verb or a place where things happen. You don't have "church." You go to church to worship, but church and worship are not interchangeable.

Worship is important, yet so many of our youth will do anything to get out of it.

Try planning a worship with your students during the youth meeting. Make the act of coming before God part of the event. Simple acts like Music, Prayer, and Communion can be done anywhere anytime. Try pulling the van over on the next field trip and worshiping at the rest stop. Browse your local used book store and find some older worship books. The Episcopal Book of Occasional Services has liturgy for worship on All Hallows Eve written in the late eighteenth century.

Worship is a powerful tool as long as it does not become always the same. Get out of the building to worship. If you can't get out of the building, worship on the roof or in the basement. If you have no basement and the administrative board would have a problem with roof-worship, change one of the rooms in the building. Pull out the furniture. Darken the windows. Light candles. By pulling the furniture out of a room that your students know well you can create new acoustics, new shadows, and a new sacred space.

You can also take worship out of the building. We had a wonderful old dude in our church. The teens loved him because he was a smart-ass. When he was in his eighties he grew tired all the time. By the time he got up on Sunday morning and got dressed he was too tired to go to church. So the youth began to take worship to him. It was just prerecorded hymns and prayers. Communion with Fritos and Coke, but it meant so much to him in the last year of his life.

**TIP #49: Worship is a powerful tool to connect your youth with God, whether they are participating or leading worship opens doors for the holy to happen.**

**50**

# The Truth Shall Make You Odd

Theologian and youth ministry guru Mike Yaconelli once wrote a piece called "You Shall Know the Truth and the Truth Shall Make You Odd."

Youth group is the place where the odd can go. Jesus ate with the outcasts he did not make them change order to have lunch with them. When we create and plan what exactly our group is at its most basic, we want a place where anyone can go and be accepted. Anyone can bring their oddness to the youth meeting.

The youth of your church have not yet become staid. They don't put on the nice clothes and sit quietly while the pastor preaches. Youth dress funny. They slouch. They pass notes. They pierce things. They always have those ear-things in their head and it sounds like a tiny belt sander. Youth think they can change the world. They know every word to certain movies and yet can't seem to memorize formulas for science class. They accept EZ-Cheese in a can as a meal.

Odd adds spice to the soup. In a world where "sameness" is celebrated, the same shall go first and the odd shall sit in the back of the room and make stupid jokes about the teacher while doodling.

Jesus did not come so that we could all be the same. Jesus came to affirm those things that make us different from everybody else.

Teens are both frightened by adulthood and screaming for it to begin. If you ask them, they'll say, "Yeah, I want to be an adult, just not the same as my mom and dad."

Sameness is the graveyard where uniqueness goes to die. When the world of sameness says, "Get what you can." Jesus says "Give."

When the world of sameness says, "Look out for number one." Jesus says, "Look out for each other."

When the world of sameness says, "Crush your enemies under your shoe and don't look back."

Jesus says, "Love your enemies. Pray for them."

The world says, "Get in line."

Jesus says, "Dance."

There's an old story, and I wish I knew where it came from. It's about a man who went to a church for the first time. He sang the hymns loudly and with fervor. When they "passed the peace" the man hugged those around him. When the pastor read the scripture the man pulled out his own Bible and read along. He even raised his hand during the sermon to ask a question! Finally, a small group of concerned members got him in a quiet place and told him that his behavior was not what they were accustomed to at their church and perhaps he would like to worship elsewhere.

Sitting outside on the step wondering what had happened the man hung his head. Jesus came by and sat next to him and said, "It's okay. I've been trying to get in there for years."

**TIP #50: Our youth groups must not only accept the oddballs and the outcasts; we should celebrate them. "You think you're the oddball? Come with us and see the power of oddballs in groups."**

# 51

## Let the Truth Do Its Own Work

"Truth" here is spelled with a capital "T". If I tell you I'd really like a cup of coffee or a pint of Ben & Jerry's right now, that would be the truth. If I want to tell you about the unconditional love of a creator and creating God who loves you like the unique and wonderful and amazing creation that you are, that would be the Truth.

Sometimes we simply have to get out of our own way. God is God. We are not. That's a hard concept for many of us. When Job stood on the mountaintop and ranted for three whole days, God said, "I'm God. You're not. Have a seat" (paraphrasing).

I could tell you what I had for supper last night (pulled pork sandwich). Last week? Not so much. I don't know what I had for dinner every Sunday last year, but I can tell you that I took nourishment from those meals. I blessed the hands that prepared them. I asked God to use them to give me strength. Your youth lessons work the same way. Can your students quote them all back to you? Probably not. Did they get something out of them? Yes, of course.

It's easy to believe your own press. You've done this for years. You can console an upset teenager and watch as he gives you kudos on his Facebook page. It's easy to have a big ego. God sent his offspring only once. We are sharing that message, and we have to remember where it came from. Sometimes we have to step back and say, "God, I'm putting this in your hands. I've counseled her, I've affirmed her, I've supported her, but she really needs you God. Please heal her."

**TIP #51: God crafted the Truth through Jesus. God's words, not ours, will make the difference.**

**52**

# Winnowing

This is going to take a minute, and it's going to go off to the side a few times, but bear with me. It'll all make sense. When I was in college I used to volunteer at the local public radio station during fund drive week. I'd take the late shift because I liked the late-night jazz DJ who looked like a convict and had a voice like Tom Waits. During the day hours all the local businesses that underwrite the station would send in gourmet food. At night we'd sit and eat platters of thick brownies and cookies and cheese that came without a date on the bottom of the can. We would also collect the bottom-of-the-bag remnants from the gourmet coffees and brew a Colombian-African-Blueberry-Hazelnut-Cocoa-Cream concoction that gave us enough of a buzz to get through some very long all-nighters.

Okay, I told you that story so I could tell you this one—about break dancers.

After a year of volunteering one of my friends and I were offered "student employment" at the station. We got to check tapes for glitches, organize sweatshirt premiums, and go along on remote recordings to wrap mike cable and peel duct tape off the floor. This was in northeast Ohio, and each year we would record the National Folk Festival. One year they decided to see if they could bring in a younger crowd by inviting some break dancers to perform. Yes, break dancers. (They called it modern folk dance.) Now in northeast Ohio, even in the summertime, you can get some wicked cold winds coming in off the lake at night. The evening of the outdoor concert the break dancers took the stage. It was a cold night, and in the glare of the stage lights you could see the steam coming off these young men as they started to move.

Okay, I told you that story so I could tell you this one—about winnowing.

Winnowing is one of those words we hear, but we never really get the idea of what it means. Winnowing was the process by which the seed is removed from the husk of the grain. All the grain was piled in what was called a "winnowing circle." Then men would go out at night to "do the winnowing". Winnowing required a wind. You could not do the winnowing in the morning because the wind came from the wrong direction (it had to come in off the water). Winnowing could not be done in the afternoon because the wind wasn't strong enough. Winnowing had to be done at night. The idea was to take your winnowing fork (picture a combination pitchfork and shovel), get a forkful of grain, and throw it into the wind. The wind then blew it back at you and you threw another forkful. You did this over and over into the wee hours of the morning, and slowly the process broke the husk off the seed. Someone else got to separate the seed and husk the next day. But the winnowers were out there all night long. You have to imagine there was some sort of winnowing song they sang to pass the time. I can also picture them in the light of lanterns or torches as their bodies started to steam in the cold wind the harder they worked.

The third chapter of Luke says that Jesus is coming, and he's bringing a winnowing fork. Try to tell me that Jesus wasn't a youth minister!

This is what youth ministry is. It requires a specific group of people to go out in the weird hours and do the work that nobody else wants to do while somebody else down the line gets credit for separating the seed from the husk.

Volunteers are out there throwing the seed into the wind over and over only to have God blow it back and say, "Try again."

Little by little they break the husk away, that shell teens use to encase themselves. It is the volunteers who break through; they sing the winnowing songs. They work into the wee hours. They sleep on floors and eat the broken cookies left on the plate. They drink the coffee that was left in the bottom of the bag, cramp themselves into church vans, and work till they are exhausted. They watch as the youth minister gets his picture in the bulletin or on the church web site.

The volunteers are out there with the winnowing forks, throwing grain into the wind over, and over hoping that something will get through. Please God, help me get through.

**TIP #52: Remember that even when it doesn't seem like it, the message gets through.**